Hook, Line, and Sinker

National Library of Canada Cataloguing in Publication

Labignan, Italo, 1955-
  Hook, line, and sinker : everything kids want to know about fishing! / Italo Labignan.

Includes index.
ISBN 1-55263-549-X

1. Fishing—Juvenile literature. I. Title.

SH445.L32 2003   j799.1   C2003-900049-4

THE CANADA COUNCIL | LE CONSEIL DES ARTS
FOR THE ARTS | DU CANADA
SINCE 1957 | DEPUIS 1957

ONTARIO ARTS COUNCIL
CONSEIL DES ARTS DE L'ONTARIO

The publisher gratefully acknowledges the support of the Canada Council for the Arts and the Ontario Arts Council for its publishing program.

We acknowledge the financial support of the Government of Canada through the Book Publishing Industry Development Program (BPIDP) for our publishing activities.

Key Porter Books Limited
Six Adelaide St. East, 10th Floor, Toronto, Ontario, Canada M5C 1H6
www.keyporter.com

Distributed in the U.S. by Publishers Group West
www.pgw.com

Design: Peter Maher

Printed and bound in China

07 08 09 10 11 5 4 3 2 1

Hook, Line, and Sinker

Everything Kids
Want to Know
about Fishing

Italo Labignan

Illustrations by Jock MacRae

KEY PORTER BOOKS

Contents

Introduction

All over the world, people who live close to the water go fishing. Whether they live in North America, Africa, or Australia, people usually don't have to go far to find a body of fresh or salt water that is full of fish.

People have been fishing for thousands of years. In many places in the world, ancient carvings and paintings on rocks show how people caught fish ages ago. Even old books, such as the Bible, tell us that people have been catching fish for a very long time.

In North America, aboriginal people used to spear salmon that were going up rivers from the sea to spawn. The people smoked or dried their catch so that they would have fish to eat in the winter.

In the Far North of North America, the Inuit and other aboriginal people of that area caught fish through the ice using a hook and line. They also speared fish.

Today, some people scuba dive in the ocean, or go snorkeling wearing a mask and fins, and use a speargun to shoot fish.

Have you ever wondered who catches the tuna that goes into the sandwiches in your lunch? Commercial anglers do. They use special boats with big nets to catch tuna, which are sold at fish markets and in stores around the world.

One important reason why people all over the world go fishing is because they enjoy it.

People like to fish because it's fun to try to trick a fish into biting some bait or a lure or a fly. When you're fishing with a hook and line and you hook a fish, it fights and tries to get off the hook. That's what sportfishing is all about—trying to hook and land a fish.

Many people also like to catch fish because they're good to eat. Fish is a very healthy food. Other people, who fish just for fun, let them go again. That's called catch and release fishing. For many people, whether they fish for food or fun, fishing is a lifelong hobby.

Fishy Fact

Some fish, like halibut and flounder, are flat and live most of their lives on the bottom of warm and cold oceans. We call these fish flatfish. When they are born they look just like other fish–their bodies are rounded and they have

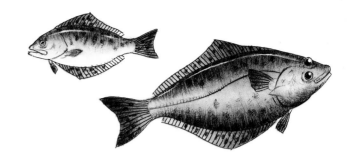

Water: A Fish's World

Our planet is mostly covered by water. Some of it—the water in oceans and seas—is salt water. Some of it—the water in rivers, streams, and lakes—is fresh water. In places where a river meets the sea, the water is a mixture of fresh and salt water. This is an estuary.

Different types of fish need different water conditions. Certain freshwater fish, such as trout, live in cold, clean rivers and streams. Usually, these waters are too cold for people to swim in. Some of the best trout fishing is in rivers and streams that begin high up in the mountains or at springs that come out of the ground. Trout and char also live in cold lakes.

In other areas, water temperatures are warmer. Warm fresh water is home for many kinds of freshwater fish, such as catfish, suckers, sunfish, crappie, carp, bass, walleye, and muskie.

More fish live in salt water than in fresh water. Oceans and seas that are close to the equator are warm all year long. Those that are closer to the poles are cold all year long. On the northern coasts of North America, you can catch many types of saltwater fish such as

an eye on either side of their heads. As they get older, their bodies flatten out like a pancake and one of their eyes moves to the same side of the head as the other eye. The under side of a flatfish is white and the upper part is camouflaged, which means that the colors on the fish's back blend in with the colors around it.

tomcod, sculpin, smelt, eel, ocean perch, mackerel, and rockfish. On the warmer, southern coasts of North America, you can catch saltwater catfish, pinfish, mackerel, sea trout, sheepshead, snapper, grouper, mullet, redfish, and snook.

No matter where you live, there is probably some body of water close to your home. It may be an ocean, river, stream, lake, pond, or canal. All of these bodies of water have different kinds of fish living in them—there's always somewhere to go fishing!

Fishy Facts

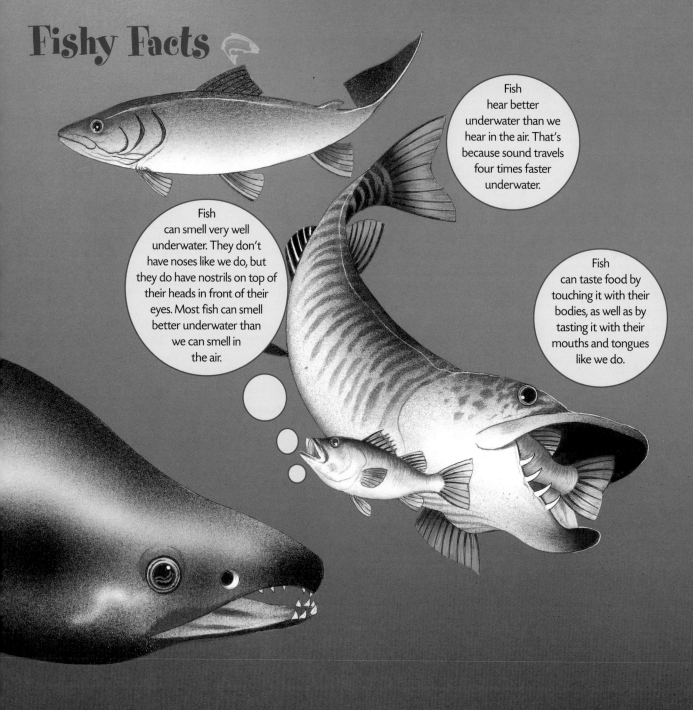

Fish hear better underwater than we hear in the air. That's because sound travels four times faster underwater.

Fish can smell very well underwater. They don't have noses like we do, but they do have nostrils on top of their heads in front of their eyes. Most fish can smell better underwater than we can smell in the air.

Fish can taste food by touching it with their bodies, as well as by tasting it with their mouths and tongues like we do.

Fish feel vibrations underwater with the sides of their bodies. If you look closely at a fish, you'll see a line running down the side of its body from the back of its head to its tail. That line is called a lateral line, and fish use it to feel vibrations when they are looking for food.

Fish can see clearly in their watery environment. Most fish have eyes near the top of their head so they can see in almost all directions, and they don't have eyelids—they sleep with their eyes wide open!

Places for Fishing

People fish in different ways and from different locations, depending on the kind of fish they are trying to catch. Some kinds of fish live in deep water lakes, others in shallow streams, and others in the ocean.

Fishing from Land

One of the easiest ways to catch fish is to fish from shore. Fish usually come close to shore looking for food. If you cast your bait or lure out from shore, there is a good chance that a fish will swim by sooner or later and find your bait. Fishing from shore takes patience because you have to wait for the fish to come to you. Try dropping your bait near sunken logs, large boulders, and trees that have fallen into the water.

Headwaters are the areas where a river or stream starts. Headwaters usually have the cleanest, coolest water in the stream or river. Fish that need very clean water, such as brook trout, live in headwaters.

If you are fishing a stream from shore, keep your eyes open for bridges and culverts (big pipes) that the water flows under or through. At those places, the stream is usually narrower and the water moves faster. Fish are attracted to fast currents. Areas where a bridge or culvert casts a shadow on the water are also good spots for fish to hide.

You can also fish from docks or piers. These structures give you the chance to fish deeper water without going out in a boat. When you fish from a dock or a pier, you can cast your bait or lure far out into the water. Try fishing under the dock, too. Fish look for food there and sometimes hide around the pilings (the supports that hold up the dock or pier).

Bridge fishing is another way of fishing from shore. From a bridge you can fish both shallow and deep water. Often big fish are attracted to the supports under the bridge because smaller fish hide around them.

Wading for Fish

Some people like to walk out into the water so that they can reach fish that are farther away from shore. If you are fishing in warm water, put on an old pair of running shoes and shorts and walk carefully into shallow water. Don't walk out into the water if you don't know what the bottom is like. Wade only where you can see the bottom and look carefully before you take a step. Never wade where the bottom is slippery or where the movement of the water might make you lose your balance.

Boat Fishing

To catch many types of fish in lakes or oceans, you have to fish from a boat. Sometimes, the fish are in a certain part of the lake or ocean. Then you can anchor the boat and let your bait go down near the bottom. You can also let the boat drift with the current. That way, you fish a bigger area. A third way is to use the motor to move the boat slowly and troll (pull your bait or lure through the water) to attract a fish.

Safety First

Before going out onto the ice to fish, the adult you are fishing with must check that the ice is safe to walk on. In some communities the police or other officials may be able to tell you if the ice in a certain area is safe.

Ice Fishing

In some parts of North America, the surfaces of lakes freeze in winter. When the ice gets thick enough to skate and walk on, many people go ice fishing. For ice fishing, you need a tool to make a hole in the ice. If the ice is not too thick, people use an ice chipper—a steel pipe with one end tapered to a thin edge about 1/2 inch (just over 1 cm) wide. To use an ice chipper, you simply lift it and let the thin edge drop onto the ice. Every time the flat edge hits the ice, it takes a chunk out of the ice. You keep doing this until the hole in the ice is big enough to pull a fish through.

If the ice is too thick for an ice chipper, people use an ice auger. This is a drill that you turn with your hands. One end of the ice auger has a sharp cutting edge. When you turn the auger, the sharp edge drills into the ice and makes a hole in it. Only use an ice chipper or auger with an adult—these tools are sharp!

When a fish takes the bait and starts tugging on the line, the twig or stick that is attached to your line will bend. This tells you when it's time to pull the fish out.

Fishing Tip

For ice fishing, you don't need a fishing rod because you can't cast your line out. Most people just hold a piece of line in their hands or attach the line to a small stick and hold that. Some people tie their lines to a small, flexible twig. They put a line down through the hole and push one end of the twig into the snow or slush beside the hole. This way you can keep your hands in your pockets to stay warm!

Fishing Tackle: What You Need to Go Fishing

Fishing tackle is the equipment you use when you're fishing. Fishing tackle stores sell many different types of rods and reels, as well as other pieces of equipment. Let's look at some of the equipment you might find, and learn a little about what you do with it.

Poles, Rods, and Reels

A fishing pole is simply a long piece of wood, such as a tree branch or piece of bamboo, with a length of fishing line the same length as the pole attached to it.

A fishing rod is manufactured. It has a handle and a reel seat, which is where a reel can be attached, and several line guides through which the fishing line is threaded up to the tip of the rod. Fishing rods are designed for a certain type of fishing reel.

A fishing reel holds the fishing line and is designed to release it when you cast the line with the bait and hook attached to it. You wind the handle on the reel to retrieve the fishing line—and a fish, if you're lucky!

Cane Pole

Cane poles are the least expensive fishing poles you can buy in a tackle store. A cane pole is a long piece of bamboo that can be divided into sections so it's easy to carry around. You attach your line to the thin end of the pole and hold the thick end. You don't need a reel. To cast your line and bait, you just swing the tip of the pole out over the water and let the bait fall into the water. When you get a bite, you lift the pole up to set the hook and flip the fish out of the water. When you're not using your pole, wrap the fishing line around it to keep the fishing line from getting tangled.

Spin Casting Rod and Reel Outfit

When you are just getting started in fishing, a spin casting rod and reel outfit is the easiest fishing outfit to use. Spin casting rods are usually made of fiberglass. The reel seat and line guides are on the upper side of the rod. With this kind of rod you use a spin casting reel, which is a closed-faced push-button reel. "Closed-faced" means that the fishing line is inside the reel so you cannot see it. This type of reel is good because the fishing line won't get tangled easily if it gets loose on the reel.

Fishing Tip

Never drop or leave your fishing rod and reel in sand or soil. If your fishing reel gets dirty, dunk it in the water to wash any grit out of it.

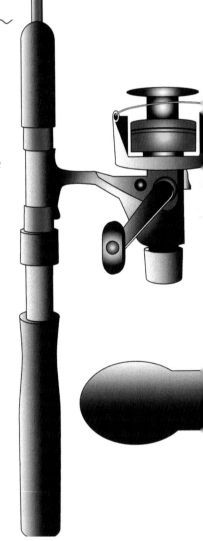

Spinning Rod and Reel Outfit

A spinning rod and reel outfit is a little more difficult to use than a spin casting rod, but you can cast farther with it. Spinning rods are usually made of fiberglass. More expensive ones are made of graphite. The reel seat and line guides are on the underside of the rod. With this kind of rod you use a spinning reel, which does not completely cover the fishing line. You have to be careful not to tangle the line if it gets loose. A spinning rod and reel outfit works well with lures.

Bait Casting Rod and Reel Outfit

A bait casting rod and reel outfit is difficult to use if you are just starting to go fishing. Bait casting rods are usually made of fiberglass or graphite. The reel seat and line guides are on the upper side of the rod. Many professional bass anglers use this outfit when they fish in bass tournaments because it allows them to cast accurately, though the line gets easily tangled.

A bait casting reel is not like other reels because the line is wound on the reel horizontally (from side to side) instead of around the reel (in a circle). For this reason, the bait casting reel is also called a level-wind reel. This type of reel allows the angler to use his or her thumb at a precise moment at the end of the casting action to stop the reel from releasing the fishing line. Beginners should not try to use a bait casting outfit when they are just starting out.

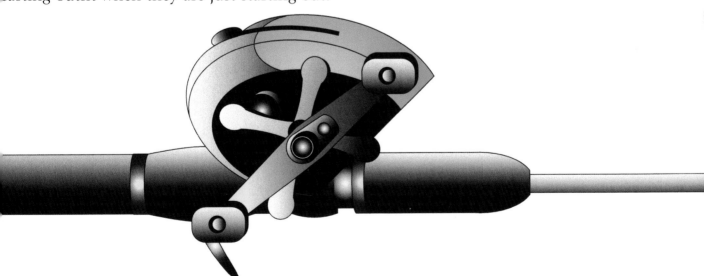

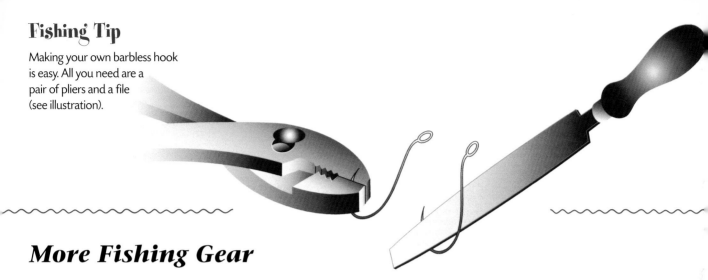

Fishing Tip

Making your own barbless hook
is easy. All you need are a
pair of pliers and a file
(see illustration).

More Fishing Gear

Hooks

Hooks come in two styles, a single hook and a treble hook. A treble
hook has three hooks at the end of the main shank. Treble hooks are
usually used on lures. Single hooks are used for fishing with bait.

Most hooks have a barb near the point of the hook. The barb is a
small piece of metal that sticks out from the shaft and points in the
opposite direction from the point. Hooks have barbs so that when
you hook a fish, the hook won't fall out. This is good if you are
planning on keeping your fish for eating because the fish won't be
able to shake the hook off. If you are practicing catch and release,
though, you should use a barbless hook. This way you won't injure
the fish when you remove the hook.

Most tackle shops sell barbless hooks and you can also buy
barbless treble hooks. You can also make your own barbless hook
with a pair of pliers. Simply "pinch-down" the barb so that it doesn't
stick out from the hook. A better way is to use a file. File down the
barb right to the shaft of the hook.

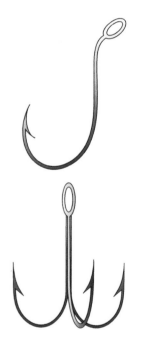

Snap Swivels

A snap swivel is a little clip that you tie to the end of your fishing line so that you can quickly attach or remove lures and hooks. Having a snap swivel on your line means you don't have to tie knots or cut your line when you want to try fishing with different lures. You just open and close the snap swivel instead. The clip is made to swivel, so as your lure spins in the water, your line doesn't get twisted.

Wire Leaders

A wire leader is a piece of wire that you attach to the end of your line. If you are going to be fishing for fish that have sharp teeth, like pike, pickerel, and muskie, you should use a wire leader. These fish can't bite through the wire.

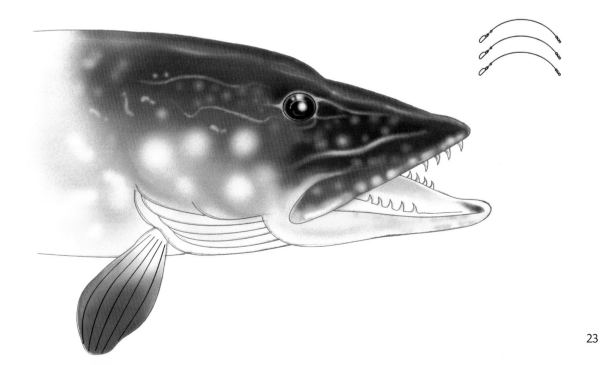

Fishing Line

Most fishing line is made from nylon and is called monofilament line. "Monofilament" means the line is a single strand, not several strands twisted together. Fishing line may be clear or different colors, such as blue, yellow, and green. All types of fishing line are thin, and some lines are stronger than others. You need stronger line if you're fishing for big fish. Companies that make fishing line mark how strong it is on the side of the spool. A number tells you the amount of weight the line can hold without breaking. For example, 4-pound-test line is a light line that you would use for catching small fish. This line will hold fish that weigh up to 4 pounds (about 2 kg) without breaking.

Tackle Box

Once you start getting some fishing lures, you will need somewhere to keep them organized and safe. You could keep them in a box, but the hooks would probably get tangled. Tackle boxes have small compartments that keep your hooks and lures separate. Tackle boxes are usually made out of plastic and come in different sizes.

If your fishing line gets tangled and you have to cut some off to get the line free, never leave the loose pieces of fishing line on the ground. Small animals and birds may become tangled and get hurt. They may even die if it prevents them from eating or from escaping from other creatures that hunt them. Always take any tangled line home and put it in the garbage.

Net

When you catch a small fish, you can probably lift it out of the water easily. If you're lucky enough to catch a bigger fish, you probably won't be able to lift it out of the water unless you use a net. Nets come in different sizes. Buy a medium-size net that has small holes in the mesh material. You can use it to land bigger fish and also to catch small insects, crayfish, minnows, and other bait.

Pocket Knife

A pocket knife is a good tool to have with you when you go fishing. You can use it to trim your knots and cut your line or pieces of bait. Make sure an adult helps you use it.

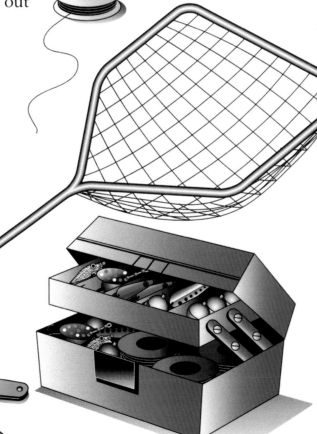

Jump In!

Make Your Own Tackle Box

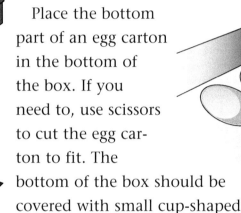

Once you start collecting hooks, sinkers, floats, and lures, you will need something to keep them in. You can make a great tackle box easily from materials you can find around the house: a cardboard shoebox, glue, a few egg cartons, and some cardboard.

To make a tackle box, first cut the lid off the egg cartons.

Place the bottom part of an egg carton in the bottom of the box. If you need to, use scissors to cut the egg carton to fit. The bottom of the box should be covered with small cup-shaped compartments. Use some glue to hold the sections of egg carton in place.

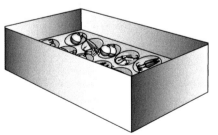

Put a different piece of fishing equipment in each egg-shaped compartment. When all the spaces are full, cut a piece of cardboard the same size as the inside of the box (a little

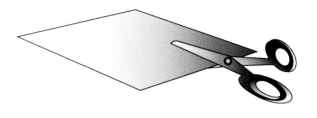

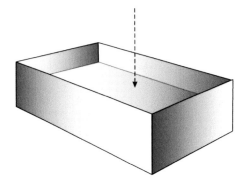

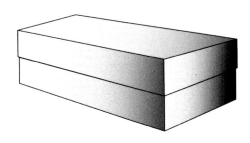

smaller than the top
of the box) and place
this on top of the
tackle in the egg

carton to keep it in place. If you need more room, add another layer
of egg carton on top of the cardboard. Put the top on the shoebox
when all your equipment is safely stored away.

When you go fishing, place your tackle box in a plastic grocery
bag with handles. The bag will make it easier to carry your box and
will also keep it dry.

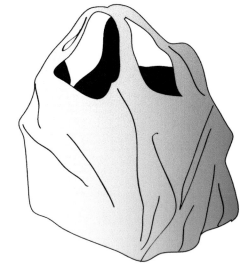

Catch bait only in places where you have permission to do so, and catch only as much as you need for your next fishing adventure. Keep your bait in the conditions it needs to stay alive. Return any live bait you don't use to where you found it or to a similar habitat (the natural living place of an animal or plant).

To safely store lures that have many hooks, stick the hooks in a small piece of styrofoam. The lure won't get tangled with other lures, and you won't get the hooks stuck in your hand.

Different Methods of Fishing

Fishing is about tricking a fish into eating whatever you've put on the hook at the end of your line. It's that simple! You can use real food—bait—that you know the fish like to eat, or you can use fake food—lures or artificial bait—that look like real fish food. Whatever you use depends on the kind of fish you are trying to catch.

Bait Fishing

For bait fishing, all you need is a small hook, some line and the right bait. There are lots of different kinds of bait. Most bait and tackle shops sell live worms, minnows (tiny fish), and shrimp, as well as frozen bait such as shrimp, herring, and sardines. Some shops also sell special live bait such as crayfish and leeches.

When you bait fish, it's important that you make the bait look natural. The more natural the bait looks, the more likely it is to attract a fish. To fish in shallow water, all you need is a pole and some bait. To fish in deeper water for fish that swim near the

bottom, you will need to put a sinker (a small weight) on your line so that your bait goes to the bottom.

If you are using a worm for bait, thread only a bit of it onto the hook. Let most of the worm dangle so that it can wiggle in the water. If you are using a minnow, hook the minnow gently through the skin or through the lower jaw so that it can still swim.

When using insects such as grasshoppers or crickets for bait, hook them gently through their body just below their neck, or thorax, from the bottom side up through the top shell. This way, they will still kick as they drift on the surface of the water. To use a shrimp for bait, hook the shrimp through the tail. When you pull the shrimp through the water, it will move the way a shrimp swims naturally.

When you do get a bite, if you are catch and release fishing, set the hook (tighten your line so that the fish gets hooked) right away. If you are planning on keeping the fish, and you have natural bait on your line, let the fish nibble for a while. Once you feel some tugging, it means the fish is trying to swim away with your bait and hook. That's the time to set the hook.

For bait fishing, you should get a flexible, or "whippy," rod. If you use a stiff fishing rod, the fish will feel it and will drop the bait before you've had a chance to set the hook!

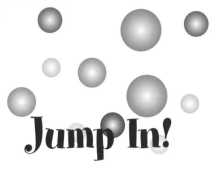

Jump In!

Catch Your Own Bait

You don't have to buy your bait from a bait shop. You can catch your own!

An easy way to find worms is to look on a sidewalk after a heavy rain. Rain makes the worms come out of the ground. If your family has a garden, you can also find worms there by digging with a small shovel. Dig in loose soil or look under rocks and logs. Most of the worms you catch this way will be small. Large worms—which are called night crawlers—come out of the ground at night. They are good bait for larger fish. If your family has a lawn, it's a great place to find night crawlers. Water your lawn just before it gets dark. When it's dark, shine a flashlight on the grass as you walk back and forth. You'll see big worms crawling out of the ground. Grab them quickly before they disappear!

The best way to keep worms is to place them in a container with a lid—a margarine container works well—with moist soil or strips of wet newspaper. Make small air holes in the lid. Keep the container in the shade while you're fishing. If you're not going fishing until the next day, keep the container in a cool spot such as on a basement floor or in the fridge. When you're fishing on a hot day, put a few ice cubes into your bait container with the worms. The melting ice cubes will keep the worms cool and lively.

Grasshoppers and crickets are good bait, too. Grasshoppers usually live in tall grass,

and crickets hide under rocks and logs. You can catch them with a small net, but you have to be fast!

Keep grasshoppers and crickets in the same kind of container you would keep worms in, and put it in a cool place overnight.

If you live close to a shallow stream or a pond, you can also use a net to catch crayfish (some people call them "crawfish") for bait. Crayfish look like tiny lobsters. They hide around and under rocks in the water. If you move a rock slowly, you may find a crayfish under or near it. Once you catch a crayfish, hold it carefully by the back so you don't get pinched by its claws.

Keep crayfish in a small lidded pail filled about one-third full with water from where you caught them.

Often you can see minnows swimming near the bank of a pond or stream. Minnows are easy to catch with a small net. Just dip it under the bank and lift the net gently out of the water. You can also buy a minnow trap at a tackle store. A minnow trap is a wire cage with small holes at each end. Minnows can swim into it, but they can't get back out. Place half a slice of bread (minnow bait!) in the middle of the trap, and put the trap underwater. Leave your minnow trap in the water all night. The next day, you should have a trap full of minnows! Keep your minnows in a bucket of water.

Float Fishing

Sometimes, it can be difficult to bait fish if there are weeds growing on the bottom, or if there are a lot of sticks, rocks, and snags such as roots, branches, or rocks beneath the surface of the water that can catch the fishing line. Your bait can get stuck. To avoid this, attach a float or bobber to your line. The float will keep your bait off the bottom so that fish can see it. When a fish starts nibbling the bait, you'll see the float move. When the float goes underwater, it's time to tighten the line and set the hook. Float fishing isn't any different from bait fishing; it's just bait fishing with a float on your line.

Floats come in different weights, shapes, colors, and sizes. Pick a brightly colored float so that you can see it easily. Floats are made of plastic or wood. Wooden floats are usually lighter than plastic floats. It is harder to cast a light float far out into the water. The good thing about light floats is that it's easier for fish to pull them under water. Plastic floats are heavier, so they are easier to cast out farther. The bad thing about heavy floats is that the fish have a harder time pulling them under water, so you may not know when you've got a bite. Always try to use a float that is heavy enough to cast, but light enough for the fish to pull under, so that the fish will not feel it when eating your bait.

Floats are useful when you are fishing for fish that don't swim along the bottom, such as sunfish, crappie, and perch.

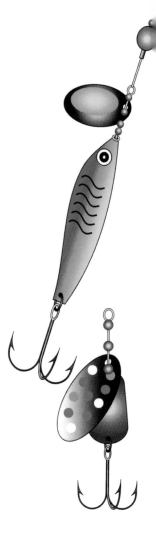

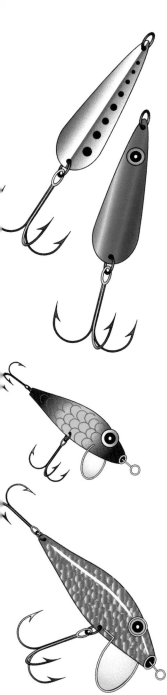

Lure Fishing

Lures are artificial bait—fake food for fish! They fool the fish into thinking they are food. Lures are a lot of fun to fish with because you have to cast them out and pull them back in over and over until you get a bite. If you let lures sit on the bottom they won't work very well.

Spoons and Spinners

There are many kinds of lures. Some are made of metal and are called spoons. Spoons are designed to look like a minnow swimming through the water. The faster you pull a spoon through the water, the more the spoon will flash and flip, and the more it will attract a fish. Spinners are also made of metal, and when you pull them through the water, they spin.

Plugs

Some lures are made of wood and look and "swim" like a small fish. These lures are called plugs. Once you've cast a plug into the water, it floats on the surface. When you pull the line in, the plug swims below the surface from side to side. If you stop reeling in, it will float back up to the surface. They are good to use for fish that swim and feed in shallow water.

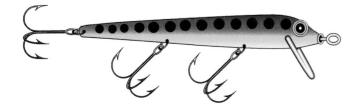

Plastic Lures and Lead Jigs

At a tackle shop, you can buy plastic worms, plastic grubs, plastic minnows, and even plastic frogs. Plastic grubs are usually used with a lead jig to help them sink to the bottom. A lead jig is a fishing hook that has a weight near the eye of the hook. This weight is often referred to as the "head" of the jig.

To fish with a weighted jig and plastic grub, cast your line out and let the lead jig and lure sink to the bottom. Then slowly reel your line in and at the same time lift your rod up. As you lift your rod up, the lure will lift off the bottom. Let it fall to the bottom again, reel more line in, and lift your rod up again. Doing this makes the lure rise and fall, which attracts fish. This method of fishing is called jigging.

Crankbaits

Some lures are made of hard plastic. These lures are usually made to look like small fish and are called crankbaits. They are designed to "swim" when they are being retrieved through the water. A piece of plastic is molded into the front of this type of lure where its "mouth" is. This piece of plastic is the "lip." As you pull the crankbait through the water, water goes over the lip and makes the crankbait swim from side to side and also makes it dive. Those with a short plastic lip are good to use for fish that live in shallow water, less than 5 feet (1.5 m) deep. Crankbaits with a longer lip are better for fish that live in deeper water, more than 5 feet (1.5 m) deep.

If you are going to be fishing mostly with lures, you need a stiffer fishing rod than you would use for bait fishing. You can cast farther

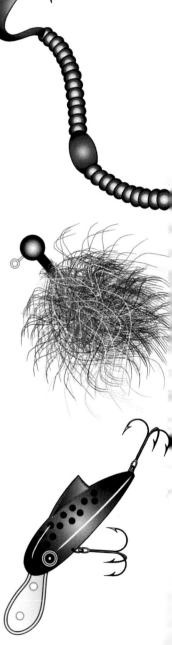

Fishing Tip

To prevent small hooks from get-ing tangled or lost in your tackle box, keep them on a safety pin. Use different sized safety pins to store different sized hooks.

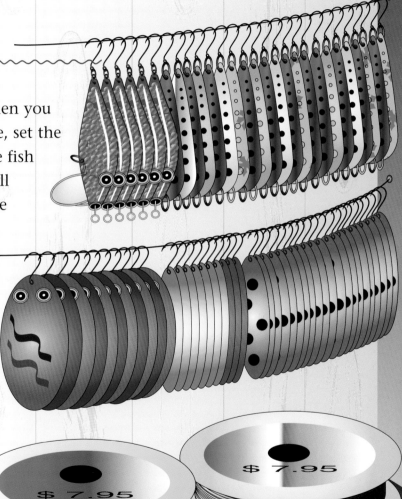

and set the hook more easily. When you are using a lure and you get a bite, set the hook right away. If you don't, the fish will let go of the lure. The fish will know within seconds that the lure is not real food.

Spoons, spinners, plugs, and crankbaits are just some of the lures you will find in a tackle store. Once you start fishing, you will probably want to buy special lures for your favorite fish.

$ 3.95

$ 7.95

$ 7.95

Jump In!

Make Your Own Floats, Sinkers, and Lures

To make a float, you'll need a cork like one that is used in a bottle.

Ask an adult to drill a small hole through the middle of the cork from the top to the bottom.

Then find a twig that will fit snugly through the hole.

Thread your line through the hole in the cork, and then slide the twig into the hole. The twig will stop the cork from sliding up or down your line.

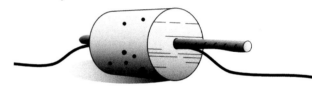

One of the easiest things to use for a sinker is a metal nut, the kind that goes on a metal bolt people use to bolt things together. You might find a metal nut in your family's toolbox. Simply tie the nut onto your fishing line below the float.

You can make your own lures using beads or costume jewelry and a piece of thin, flexible wire about 4 inches (10 cm) long. If you don't have a piece of wire, a twist-tie from your kitchen will work well, too. Remove the paper or plastic from the twist-tie before you begin.)

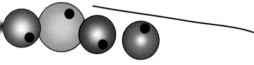

First, make a small loop at one end of the wire and twist it so that the loop is secure. You'll tie your fishing line to this loop.

Next, thread some beads of different sizes onto the wire. Thread a hook onto the end of the wire, and then twist the wire so that the beads and hook cannot slip off.

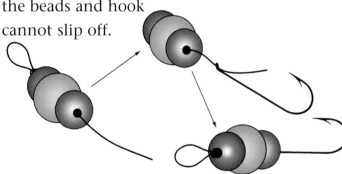

That's it! Making lures is quick and easy. Try using beads of different shapes, sizes, and colors to make your lures. Keep track of which lures the fish like best.

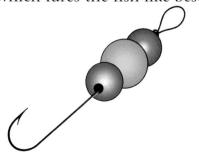

Fishing Tip

In most places, kids won't need a fishing license, but adults will. Adults should find out about the fishing regulations for their area from the provincial or state government.

Fishing Step by Step

Once you've got some basic fishing equipment, go fish!

When you're a beginner, it's best to try fishing from shore first. (You can try fishing from a boat when you have more experience.) Find an area near the water where you can stand safely—a grassy bank, a beach, some small rocks along the shore, or a dock or pier. Pick a spot away from bushes, tall grass, or trees that might get in the way when you try to cast your fishing line out.

Use either a simple fishing pole, a spin casting rod and reel outfit, or a spinning rod and reel outfit. For bait, use worms, which are easy to get and are good bait for many kinds of fish. Add a sinker to weight your line, and a float to keep your hook off the bottom and show you when you've got a bite.

You do three main things when you're fishing: bait your hook, cast, and land your catch. Let's look at each of these actions step by step.

Fishing Tip

If you are fishing in a small stream or canal, try dropping your bait below an undercut bank where fish like to hide, or in the areas where the stream or canal makes a bend and the current has dug out the bottom and made the water deeper.

Baiting a Hook

Baiting a hook is easy.

1. Pick a wiggly worm from your container. Hold it between the thumb and first finger of one hand. Make sure you hold it tightly so that it can't squirm away, but not so tightly that you squish it!

2. Hold the hook between the thumb and the first finger of your other hand. Gently put the hook through one end of the worm. To make sure the worm stays on the hook, put the hook through the worm at least one more time. Leave some of the worm dangling off the hook. (If you leave too much dangling, a fish can easily eat it without getting hooked.)

Casting

Now you need to get your line and bait into the water. Stand safely close to the water. Keep your legs slightly apart so that you are well balanced and won't slip. Before you cast, make sure your hook is not near your body and that you have enough room around you so you won't hook other people.

Casting with a Fishing Pole

Casting with a fishing pole is a little easier than casting with a rod and reel outfit.

1. Hold the pole so that the tip of it points to the sky.
2. Swing the pole so that the line, float, sinker, and bait go out over the water and let them fall into the water.

Once you've cast, hold the fishing pole parallel to the surface of the water so that you have some loose line. If you don't leave some line loose, when a fish bites it will feel the resistance of the rod and probably let go of the bait.

Fishing Tip

If you are fishing for fish with small mouths, use a small hook and only a little piece of bait. If you run out of bait, share your lunch! Roll a piece of bread into a ball and put it on your hook. You can also use scraps of lunch meat for bait.

41

Casting with a Spin Casting or a Spinning Rod and Reel Outfit

You can cast farther out from the shore when you use a rod and reel outfit.

1. Before you cast, make sure the float is about 6 inches (15 cm) away from the tip of the rod. If you need to, reel in some line by turning the handle on the reel.

2. If you are using a spin casting reel, push the button down with your thumb and hold it down. If you are using a spinning reel, hold the fishing line directly in front of the reel against the rod with your index finger. With your other hand, flip the casting bail over to the open position.

3. Slowly move the fishing rod back over your shoulder so that the tip of the rod is pointing behind you.

4. If you are using a spin casting reel, swing the rod behind you as you continue to hold down the button. As you swing the rod in front of you, release the button. This allows the fishing line to be cast out in front of you. If you are using a spinning reel, swing the rod from behind you to in front of you so that the fishing line is released in front of you.

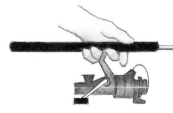

Eco-Alert

Fry are very young fish that are less than 2 inches (5 cm) in length. Never keep undersize fish. Check your local fishing regulations for the legal size of the fish you want to catch.

Fishing Tip

When you're casting with a rod and reel, the faster you flip the rod forward from over your shoulder, the farther out your line will go.

5. Once your bait, sinker, and float hit the water, reel in some of the loose line. Hold the fishing rod parallel to the surface of the water.

Landing Your Catch

You'll know when a fish has taken the bait when you feel a tug on the line and the float starts bobbing. Now you have to land your catch.

1. Let the fish pull the float under the surface of the water.

2. Pull or reel in the line until it tightens, and lift the tip of the pole or rod so that it points toward the sky. Now you've hooked the fish.

3. If you're using a rod and reel outfit, reel in the line until the fish is close to shore.

4. Lift the fish onto the bank or dock.

What to Do with the Fish You Catch

When you catch a fish, you can either let it go or take it home to eat. Either way, you must first remove the hook.

Catch and Release Fishing

If you love the sport of fishing, you should respect the fish and the environment in which they live. Once you start catching fish, you should always release more than you take home.

Fish that are to be released should be released properly if they are to survive. There are many things you can do to ensure fish you are catching and planning to release have a good chance of surviving.

Try and use an artificial lure as often as possible. When fish grab lures, they usually know that they are not real, so they don't swallow them. Or, if you are using live bait and you get a bite, don't let the fish swallow the bait. Set the hook quickly so the fish will only be

hooked in the mouth, not in the throat or stomach. You should also use the largest hook you can find so that the fish can't swallow the hook.

Fishy Facts

Small fish have to beware of being eaten by larger fish. Most small fish can swim very fast and dart away from a hungry bigger fish. The blowfish is a small fish that lives in the shallow water of warm oceans. It can't swim fast. If a larger fish gets close to it, the blowfish fills itself with air just like a balloon so that it looks too big for another fish to swallow. When the bigger fish swims away, the blowfish lets out the air and shrinks down to its normal size.

Some fish are very clever when it comes to catching their favorite food. The archer fish lives near the island of Java in Indonesia. This fish eats insects that crawl on the branches and weeds hanging over the water. The hungry archer fish fills its mouth with water, slowly swims to the surface beneath the insect and then spits the water through the air to knock the insect into the water. Fast food!

Believe it or not, some fish go fishing for fish they like to eat. The angler fish lives in some of the deepest parts of the oceans. It has a built-in fishing rod that sticks out of the top of its head. At the end of this thin rod there is a small clump that looks like bait to a small fish. The angler fish lies behind a rock and shakes its thin rod until a small fish gets close to the small dangling clump. When it gets close enough, the angler fish opens its mouth and has a tasty meal.

Removing the Hook and Letting Your Fish Go

Dip your hands in the water before you touch a fish. If your hands are dry, they will take the slime off the fish where you touch it. The slime is important to the fish because it protects it from infection, just as our skin protects us.

If you are going to release the fish you have caught, be as gentle as possible when you are handling it and removing the hook. Be careful not to touch the eyes or gills of a fish, which are very sensitive. Try not to drop the fish: its eyes may get scratched on the ground, and its slime may come off on the dirt or grass.

Keep the fish in the water while you remove the hook. Remember that fish cannot breathe when they are out of water. If you have to hold the fish out of the water, take the hook out as quickly as possible, then get it back in the water so it can breathe. If you have pliers with you, try to remove the hook with the pliers without touching the fish with your hands.

Always let a fish revive before you release it. If you have caught a

...arger fish and it is tired from fighting after you remove the hook, hold it by the tail in the water until it gets its strength back before you release it. You will know a fish has its strength back when it swims out of your hand by itself.

To remove a hook, you have to slide it out of the fish backwards—the opposite way the hook went into the fish. If your hook has a barb, you may have to move it carefully back and forth to get the barb to slip back through the hole through which it entered.

If the fish has swallowed your hook and bait, don't try to pull the hook out. Doing so will hurt the fish. Instead, just cut the line close to the mouth of the fish and let it go.

When you have removed the hook, gently hold the fish in the water until it swims away. If you are fishing from a bridge or a dock, gently toss the fish back into the water.

Eco-Alert

! Keep only as many fish as
you and your family are
going to eat.

Keeping Your Fish for Eating

Fish are healthy food and they taste great! If you are going to eat
the fish you catch, the best thing to do is to put it in a cooler filled
with ice.

Never keep fish in a plastic bag unless you are going to put the fish
in a cooler with ice. If you're not using a cooler, keep your fish in a
cool, shady spot in the open air, such as under a tree or on some
grass or moss. Never keep them in the hot sun where they may spoil.

You may like eating fish so much that you keep most of the fish
you catch. Then you may want to buy a creel. A creel is a small bas-
ket made of soft branches. It has straps so you can hang it from your
shoulder as you are walking and fishing. The lid opens and closes
but also has a small hole in it for you to slide a fish through. Put
some wet moss, leaves, or grass in the bottom of the creel. That way,
your fish will stay cool and fresh until you get home.

Always be very careful when you are using a knife. Make sure the blade is facing away from you and will not cut you if your hand slips. Keep your pocket knife closed when you are not using it.

Cleaning Fish

Once you get your fish home, there are two easy ways to clean it. First you will need some newspapers to lay the fish on and a sharp knife such as a pocket knife or fish filleting knife. Fishing tackle stores sell filleting knives and special fish cleaning gloves that protect your hands from cuts. These gloves are made of Kevlar and stainless steel, which the knife won't cut through if it slips as you're using it. Always have an adult help you clean your fish.

Scaling, Gutting, and Gilling Fish

Some people like to clean their fish so that it stays in one piece with the head and skin on. When it's time to cook the fish, it can be cut into smaller pieces so that it cooks faster.

First you have to remove the scales from the fish. You can use a dull knife to do this. A butter knife works well, but a fish scaler works better. Fish scalers, which are available at tackle shops, are made of plastic and have a serrated edge for scraping the scales off the fish. Start scaling the fish near the head by pushing the dull knife or fish scaler against the scales all the way down to the tail.

The scales will pop off. Once you have completed one side of the fish, flip it over and do the other side. When you're done, wipe the fish off with newspaper and clean up the loose scales. Now you're ready for gutting.

Lay the fish on its side and stick the tip of the knife into its belly with the cutting edge facing away from you. You don't have to put the knife in too far—just under the skin is fine. Carefully slide the knife all the way up to the gills. Cut around the edge of the gills and detach them from the body and head. You can now remove them and the guts at the same time with your fingers. Use your knife to scrape off any blood along the inside of the fish's backbone. Rinse the fish with water, and then pat it dry with paper towel.

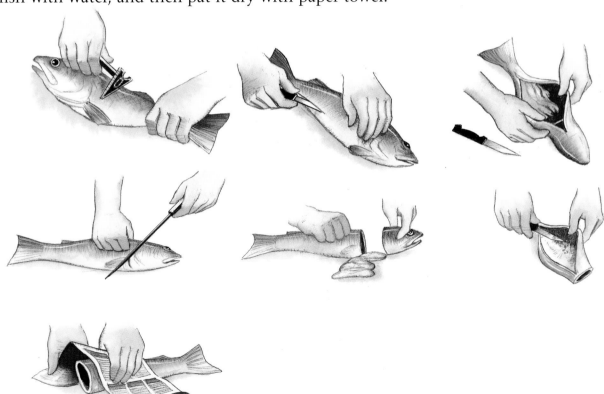

Fishy Facts

Monster Fish! Most people consider a fish that weighs only a few pounds to be a good catch, but some huge fish have been caught around the world. Many are so big they become world records (until the next monster fish is caught!). The International Game and Fish Association (IGFA) keeps a record of these large catches.

The largest fish ever caught on a single line was a 2,664-pound (1,208- kg) white shark caught by Alfred Dean in Australia in 1959. Now that's one big fish!

The IGFA also keeps records for each species of fish caught by girls and boys in two age categories: "Small Fry" (under 10 years old) and "Junior" (ages 11 to 16). Here are the records for walleye:

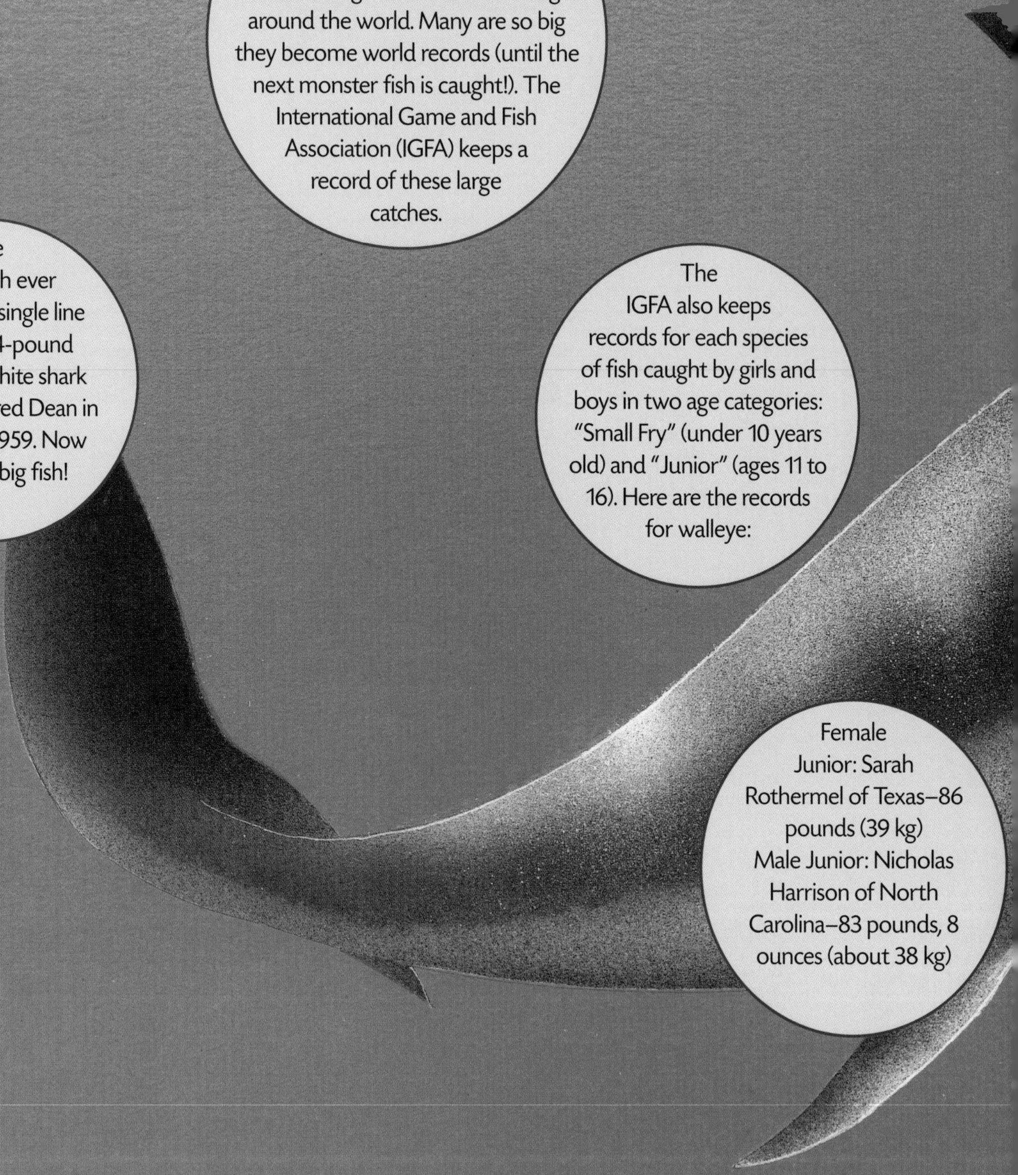

Female Junior: Sarah Rothermel of Texas—86 pounds (39 kg)
Male Junior: Nicholas Harrison of North Carolina—83 pounds, 8 ounces (about 38 kg)

Female
Small Fry: Sarah Black of the Bahamas—39 pounds, 8 ounces (about 18 kg)

Male
Small Fry: Zane Southwick of Fiji (in the South Pacific)—58 pounds, 6 ounces (about 26 kg)
The next time you drop your line into the water, something big—really big—could happen!

Jump In!

Tie Your Own Knots

To fish, you have to know how to tie a few knots. Here are some simple knots you can use to tie your hooks, lures, snap swivels, and wire leaders to your fishing line. After tying any of these knots, always leave about 3/4 inch (about 2 cm) of line when you trim the excess line so that the knot won't come undone.

The Half Hitch
The half hitch is the most common knot used to tie a hook or lure to the fishing line. Here's how to tie a half hitch:

1. Thread about 4 to 6 inches (10 to 15 cm) of line through the eye of the hook or lure.

2. Take the end of the line you threaded through the eye and make a loop with the main line. The hook or lure should be on the line, inside the loop.

3. Pass the end of the line through the loop you just made.

4. Hold and pull both the free end and the line attached to the rod—the half hitch will tighten.

If you are going to use this knot, you must tie at least three half hitches, one after the other, so that they won't come loose. The half hitch is not as strong as the Palomar and clinch knots.

The Palomar Knot

The Palomar knot is one of the easiest fishing knots to use when you want to tie a single hook to the line. Here's how to tie the Palomar knot:

1. Double about 4 to 6 inches (10 to 15 cm) of line and thread the doubled line through eye of the hook.

2. Make a half hitch (see the instructions above), but don't tighten it.

3. Place the loop of doubled line over the hook.

4. To tighten the knot, pull the line that goes to your fishing rod.

The Clinch Knot

The clinch knot is another easy knot that is used for tying hooks, snap swivels, or wire leaders to fishing line. Here's how to tie the clinch knot:

1. Thread about 4 to 6 inches (10 to 15 cm) of line through the eye of the piece of equipment you want to attach.

2. Take the line that you have threaded through the eye and twist it six times around the main line above the eye.

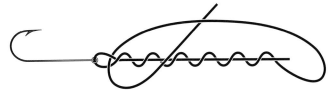

3. Thread the free end of the line through the loop that is formed where the line goes through the eye.

4. Pull the line that goes to your rod, and the clinch knot will tighten.

Know Your Fish: An Illustrated Guide

Let's take a look at the different types of fish you might catch. The kind of fish you catch depends on the body of water that you are fishing in, such as cold or warm oceans or lakes, streams, and rivers.

Legend: B—bait fishing; L—lure fishing; F—fly fishing

Cold Freshwater Fish

Common Sucker [B]
Many different kinds of suckers live in the cold rivers, streams, and lakes of North America. These fish are bottom feeders: their mouths are on the underside of their heads and they use them like a vacuum cleaner to suck up small plants and animals that live on the bottom. Suckers also feed on worms and insects that fall into the water.

Brown Trout [B, L, F]
The brown trout is a European trout that was brought to North America by the early settlers. Today, brown trout can be caught almost anywhere in the northern part of North America. Many fishers believe that the brown trout is the smartest and the hardest trout to catch. It often hides under stream banks, floating logs, and tree roots that are growing in the water. Brown trout eat the same food as the other trout and often look for food at night.

Lake Trout [B, L]
Lake trout live in the coldest, deepest parts of lakes and grow to very large sizes. These fish can be found in most cold-water lakes in the northern part of North America. In the summer, they can be caught in deep water (more than 100 feet or 30 m deep). The easiest time to catch lake trout is in the spring when they look for food in shallow water. During the spring, you can catch lake trout simply by casting lures from the shoreline. Lake trout eat small fish.

Rainbow Trout [B, L, F]
Rainbow trout live in areas of deep water in cold lakes and the fast water and rapids of streams and rivers in northwestern North America. This species has been introduced in other parts of North America and throughout the world. Rainbow trout are beautifully colored and were given their name because when they jump out of the water when they are hooked they look like a rainbow. They eat insects, small fish, worms, and trout and salmon eggs.

Dolly Varden Char [B, L, F]
A dolly varden char looks a lot like a brook trout but lives only in the rivers, streams, and lakes of the northwestern part of North America. Just like the brook trout, the dolly varden char needs cold, clean water to survive. This species eats the same foods as other trout—insects, small fish, salmon eggs, and worms.

Warm Freshwater Fish

Catfish [B]

Catfish can be found in most warm-water rivers, streams, lakes, and ponds. They get their name from the whiskers that stick out from the side of their heads like a cat's whiskers do. Catfish are bottom feeders, like carp, and they use their whiskers to taste food as they swim close to the bottom. Catfish will eat almost anything, but especially prefer dead fish and anything smelly. Catfish have sharp spines on their backs, on both sides of their bodies, and on their fins. If you ever catch a catfish, handle it carefully so that you don't get pricked!

Sunfish [B, L, F]

Sunfish are one of the most common fish found in warm-water ponds and lakes. Sunfish have bright yellow, green, blue, orange, and red markings. This species lives in the shallow part of lakes and ponds and eats insects and worms. While they are one of the easiest fish to catch, like catfish, sunfish have sharp spines on their fins and must be handled carefully.

Crappie [B, L, F]

Crappie are found in the same warm-water rivers, streams, lakes, and ponds as sunfish. Crappie are often near underwater weeds in areas where trees have fallen into the water. These fish swim around together in schools. So, when you catch one crappie, chances are good that you'll catch more. Crappie eat insects, worms, and small fish, but also bite at small lures. Many people like to ice fish for crappie in the winter. Like catfish and sunfish, crappie have sharp spines in their fins, so hold them by the lower jaw, not by the body.

Rock Bass [B, L, F]

Rock bass live in the same bodies of water as sunfish and crappie. This species got its name because it swims and feeds around rocks and boulders. Rock bass eat crayfish but can also be caught using worms, minnows, and small lures. Be careful when you hold a rock bass because they also have sharp spines on their fins.

Perch [B, L, F]

Perch are bright yellow fish with dark stripes going down the sides of their bodies. Perch swim in shallow and deep water and feed on smaller fish. This species is also attracted to small lures. It is a popular type of fish to catch in the winter when ice fishing.

Largemouth Bass [B, L, F]

Largemouth bass are probably the most popular gamefish (a species of fish that has daily catch limits and a definite open and closed season) in North America. There are many fishing tournaments where fishers compete to catch the heaviest largemouth bass. Largemouth bass live in the shallow water around lily pads and tree stumps and eat crayfish, minnows, frogs, and worms.

Smallmouth Bass [B, L, F]

Sometimes smallmouth bass and largemouth bass can be found in the same lakes, rivers, and streams. Smallmouth bass live in deep water where there are lots of rocks and can often also be found living in lakes that are too cold for largemouth bass. Smallmouth bass eat crayfish, minnows, and leeches. Once they are hooked, smallmouth bass may jump out of the water.

Pike [B, L, F]

You can always tell you've caught a pike because it is an unusual looking fish, bright green with markings that run along the sides of its body. These fish are also very long and may weigh up to 50 pounds (about 22 kg). Watch out for their sharp teeth! Pike live in the shallow water around weeds where they wait for small fish to swim by; when one comes near, the pike swims out from its hiding place and eats the small fish. Pike are easy to catch with lures.

Pickerel [B, L, F]

Pickerel live in warm, shallow, weedy water. They look like pike but are smaller. Pickerel eat minnows and are easy to catch with lures.

Walleye [B, L]

Walleye is another popular gamefish in northern North America. Many people like to eat walleye because they don't taste very fishy. Walleye often feed after dark and usually swim close to the bottom looking for minnows, crayfish, leeches, and worms. Walleye swim together in schools, so if you catch one you will probably catch more. The best way of fishing for walleye is from a boat.

Muskie [B, L]

"Muskie" is the short name for "muskellunge." This is one of the largest fish you can catch in a warm-water river or lake. Muskie are shaped like pike and pickerel and have vertical markings on the sides of their bodies. This species can grow to weigh over 70 pounds (about 32 kg). It has lots of large teeth for catching and eating other fish. To catch muskie, you can use either lures or large fish such as suckers as bait.

Cold Saltwater Fish

Tomcod [B, L]

Tomcod live in and around shoreline rocks and the pilings of piers in the cold Pacific and Atlantic Oceans. Tomcod spend most of their time swimming along the bottom looking for food. They have small whiskers on their lower jaw that they use, like catfish do, for tasting. Tomcod eat worms, molluscs, squid, and smaller fish. On the Atlantic coast, tomcod are caught by ice fishing.

Sculpin [B, L]

Sculpin live in the shallow cold water of the Pacific Ocean of northwestern North America. They swim and look for food near rocks and piers. Sculpin eat worms, small crabs, and small fish but can be caught easily using mussels and clams or a small piece of herring for bait. They can also be caught using small lures.

Smelt [B, L]
Smelt live in the cold Pacific and Atlantic Oceans, but have also migrated to the Great Lakes. Smelt, which are very tasty fish, come close to shore in the winter and when they spawn. Many people catch smelt with nets when they are spawning. Smelt can also be caught using small minnows, pieces of herring, or small lures. People go ice fishing for smelt, too.

Rockfish [B, L]
Many kinds of rockfish live in the cold waters of the Pacific and Atlantic Oceans. Some people call rockfish "rockcod." Rockfish can be many different colors and sizes. These fish live near the bottom around rocks and weeds. Rockfish can be caught easily using herring or sardines as bait, or with lures.

Flounder [B, L]
Flounder is a type of flatfish. Like other flatfish, a flounder has both eyes on the same side of its head. Flounder live in both cold and warm areas of the Atlantic Ocean off the east coast of North America. The best way to catch flounder is to use a piece of fish or shrimp for bait and drop your line close to the bottom.

Warm Saltwater Fish

Sheepshead [B]
Sheepshead are lazy fish that slowly feed on barnacles growing on pilings under piers and elsewhere. This species lives in the warm Atlantic Ocean and swims around in bays and canals. Sheepshead have silver and white sides with bright black stripes. If you walk along a dock, keep your eyes open: it's common to see sheepshead feeding near the pilings just below the surface of the water. Sheepshead eat clams, oysters, crabs, and shrimp.

Snapper [B, L]
Snapper is a very popular saltwater gamefish of warm oceans. Snapper live near rocks and coral. They also hide among the roots of mangrove trees that grow along the edges of warm ocean waters. Snapper eat small fish and shrimp. When you hook a snapper, it puts up a good fight.

Snook [B, L, F]
Snook live in warm oceans and can be caught close to shore and in water up to 30 feet (9 m) deep. These fish cruise through shallow water along shorelines bordered by mangroves in search of shrimp, small crabs, and small fish. Snook can often be found near trees that are in the water, at the mouths of saltwater creeks and channels, and around bridge and pier abutments. You can catch snook with live bait fish and shrimp or lures, such as spoons, plugs, and surface lures. One of the best times to catch big snook is at night.

Index